THE SNAPSHOT

FOR MY HUSBAND

AUTHOR / PICTURES / COVER

TANJA FEILER

INTRO AND THE SCREENPLAY "AMERICAN STORY"

THE STORY SO FAR: SAMMY, WHO HAS ONE YEAR LOOKED AFTER IN A DISTANT LAND TO CHILDREN IN NEED, HAS AMBASSADOR KIRA BIEN ACQUAINTED WITH HIS WORK, A CELEBRITY DESIGNATED FILM ACTRESS AND HER HUSBAND NICK

SICK. NOT MANY WORDS: SAMMY AND CELEBRITIES, ACTORS WANT TO RETURN TRAVEL TO PET CITY, THERE TO PLAY A MOVIE WHOSE PLOT IS COMPLETELY UNKNOWN. KIRA HAS BEEN RECALLED BY A CONVERSATION WITH SAEMMY AT SOMETHING SHE HAS STRESSED FOR YEARS, AND HAS LEARNED FROM THE CUTE PETS AND ALIEN. PROMPT WAS PACKED, THE TEN HOUR FLIGHT TOOK SAMMY AND THE COUPLE FOR THE . DAS

COUPLE NICK SICK WILL PRODUCE THE FILM THEMSELVES AND TAKE CARE OF EVERYTHING, WHICH IS IMPORTANT AS AN ACTOR IN HOLLYWOOD.

THIS ITEM CHARGED KIRA A LONG TIME, AUTHOR UNKNOWN. THIS LIES.

SHE READS IT FROM THE CUTE PETS WHOSE ENGLISH SKILLS ARE OK. BUT FOR SAFETY'S SAKE YOU STILL USE A ONLINE TRANSLATOR IN GERMAN. KIRA READS,

AND ALL OF THE COMMUNITY ARE HERE.

KILA BIEN IS A SPACE ALIEN: WE HAVE THE PROOF

A MAN CLAIMS HE WAS ABDUCTED BY AN ALIEN SPACESHIP. WHAT I FIND INTERESTING ABOUT HIS STORY IS WHEN HE STATES THE ROOM IN THE SPACECRAFT IN WHICH HE WAS PLACED WAS FULL OF KIRA BIEN POSTERS. THIS HAS US, AT THE

IRRATIONAL INQUIRER, THINKING. THIS STORY LEADS TO FOUR POSSIBILITIES:

1.) KIRA BIEN LITERALLY HAS UNIVERSAL BEAUTY. SHE IS POPULAR ON EARTH AND OTHER PLANETS. HER AGENT SHOULD BE DISCUSSING UNIVERSAL ROYALTY RIGHTS ON THOSE ALIEN POSTERS. ALTHOUGH, WE ARE NOT CERTAIN IS THIS MAY

CAUSE CURRENCY CONVERSION PROBLEMS.

2.) THE ALIENS WANT ABDUCTEES TO FEEL COMFORTABLE AND AT HOME. THIS LEADS TO THE QUESTION OF WHY THE ALIENS CHOSE KIRA BIEN POSTERS TO PLACE IN THE HUMAN EVALUATION ROOM. IS THIS HOW DISTANT CIVILIZATIONS VIEW US, AS KIRA BIEN WORSHIPPERS? I AM NOT SAYING THIS VIEW IS WRONG, I AM JUST

SURPRISED ALIENS FROM OTHER GALAXIES ARE ABLE TO REALIZE THIS.

3.) THE POSTERS JUST HAPPENED TO BELONG TO ONE OF THE ALIENS. MAYBE THE REASON ALIENS COME TO EARTH IS TO COLLECT POSTERS. DO OTHER ROOMS HAVE POSTERS OF FARRAH AND DEREK JETER AND OTHERS? DO THEY JUST COLLECT POSTERS, OR DO THEY WATCH THE

MOVIES AND FOLLOW OUR SPORTS TEAMS AS WELL?

4.) THE MAN IN NUTS.

OUR IMMEDIATE QUESTION IS, REGARDLESS OF WHICH OF FOUR HYPOTHESES IS CORRECT, WHY KIRA BIEN? WHY NOT, SAY, JADE PETTERSON? IS THE GREAT COSMIC QUESTION, THE REASON FOR ALL UNIVERSAL FORMATION HAS BEEN IN EXISTENCE

FOR IS TO ANSWER THE ONE ULTIMATE QUESTION: WHO NICK SICK SHOULD BE WITH?

THEN THE TRUTH OCCURRED TO US. KIRA BIEN IS A SPACE ALIEN. SHE CAME TO CONQUER EARTH. FORTUNATELY, IN ALIEN DEFINITIONS, CONQUERING A PLANET DOES NOT MEAN MILITARY CONQUEST BUT SOCIETAL CONQUEST. WE INDEED HAVE BECOME A PLANET THAT BOWS DOWN

AND GIVES OUR MONEY TO KIRA BIEN.

WE NOTE KIRA BIEN HAS ALL THE TRAITS OF A SPACE ALIEN. WHEN SHE WAS CAUGHT WEARING A VIAL OF A HUMAN BEING BLOOD AROUND HER NECK, THAT WASN'T SOME KINKY ROMANTIC GESTURE. SHE WAS COLLECTING EARTH SAMPLES. REMEMBER WHEN SHE WAS CAUGHT KISSING HER "BROTHER" IN PUBLIC? NO EARTHLING WOULD DO

THAT, WELL, AT LEAST NOT IN PUBLIC. SHE HAS LIONS GUARDING HER HOUSE. THIS HAD US STUMPED UNTIL WE REALIZED THE OBVIOUS: SHE IS A SPACE ALIEN. SHE HAS SOME KIND OF ABILITY TO CONTROL THE ACTIONS OF ANIMALS, OTHERWISE SHE WOULD RISK GOING OUT TO CHECK THE MAIL AND BEING DEVOURED.

WE EARTHLINGS HAVE FALLEN UNDER THE TRANCE OF KIRA BIEN. NO MATTER

HOW BAD HER MOVIES ARE, WE KEEP SCREAMING FOR MORE. WHEN SHE WAS APPOINTED GOODWILL AMBASSADOR", LITTLE DID WE KNOW IT WAS AN AMBASSADOR FOR A DISTANT PLANET. TAKE US, KIRA, WE ARE YOURS.

P.S. ANY TIME YOU WISH TO VISIT AND PROBE US, WE'RE AVAILABLE. WE JUST HOPE YOU ALREADY HAVE ENOUGH BLOOD SAMPLES.

AUTHOR UNKNOWN, PUBLISHED FOR ALL.

THE CUTE PETS WERE ALL UPSET ABOUT SUCH NONSENSE. ALIEN HAS IS THE KIRA AND NICK FROM A MACHINE IN A LABORATORY WHERE HE MAY BORROW FROM TIME TO TIME. THIS MACHINE IS THE PROTOTYPE, FOR TWO HOURS, THE ROOM IS TRANSFORMED IN THE ATMOSPHERE, AS IF YOU WERE ON THE BEACH, OCEAN WITH PALM TREES,

PERFECT. THE TWO PACKS THE CURIOSITY, KIRA NICK INFORMED ABOUT THE PLOT OF THE FILM, AND IN HOUR, THE SCRIPT IS READY. THE ACTOR MARRIED COUPLE IS SURPRISED THAT NOT AS USUAL HYSTERIA OR STARDOM HAS NO TRACE OF A FAN.

SICK NICK HAS INFORMED HOLLYWOOD AND EVERYTHING IS NECESSARY FOR THE FILM TO ART, EQUIPMENT. NICK, AS HE PRODUCED SOME OF

HIS FILMS THEMSELVES, THEIR OWN STUDIOS, CINEMATOGRAPHERS, ART AND SINCE THE FILM WILL PLAY IN PET CITY. HOLLYWOOD IS ENTHUSIASTIC ABOUT THE CONTENT AND GIVEN AN AIRPLANE WITH NEAT SPEED, SO ALL THE NEXT DAY BECAUSE WAS. WITH A CLICK ON THE OFFICIAL SITE OF CUTE PETS KNOW KIRA AND NICK THE BASIC INFORMATION, KIRA FEELS WELL IN THE WG, THE THING AND MOST THAT THEY ARE

FIGHTING MORE THAN TEN YEARS FOR A SOCIAL PROJECT THAT FOUNDERED ON THE POLITICAL SYSTEM OF THE CITY. BUT ALL DO NOT GIVE UP AND SINCE THE CUTE PETS SATURDAYS ALWAYS HAVE THEIR TALK THERAPY, THERE IS NO EXCITEMENT, EVERYONE HAS TO FIND ENOUGH TIME ABOUT HERSELF AND THE COUPLE SICK.

THE EMPLOYEE NICK SICKS ARE ALL DISCREETLY

ARRIVED IN PET CITY, PACKED WITH CAMERAS, AND A LOT OF TECHNOLOGY.

THE ACTION TAKES PLACE OFF THE PREMISES OF THE WG.

GOOD PET IS STUDENT PLAY THE ROLE OF WHO IS PLANNING A BLOODBATH WREAK IN HIS SCHOOL. ACTION:

IT POUNDED IN HIS HEAD, HE DID NOT UNDERSTAND THE

LYRICS. BUT THIS BAND FROM GERMANY WITH THEIR HARSH SOUND HAD DRAWN HIM INTO ITS SPELL. HE WAS A LONER, SHY, BLASPHEMED THE CLASSMATES ABOUT HIM, HE COULD HEAR HER WHISPERING EVEN WHEN THEY ARE NOT NEAR HIM WARE. THEN THERE WAS FOR HIM ONLY ONE THING: LOUD METAL TO HEAR. HIS PARENTS WERE BOTH EMPLOYED, HE HAD SINCE EARLY CHILDHOOD MOST OF THE TIME ALONE. TV,

MUSIC AND VIDEO GAMES, WHICH WERE HIS FRIENDS. BUT ON THIS DAY HE HAD A HEADACHE HELLISH. HE WENT INTO THE DRUGSTORE, BOUGHT HIS TABLETS, BUT NOT REALLY HELPED. THE VIOLENT GAMES ON PC ÖDETEN HIM, SOCIAL NETWORKS HE MEIDETE BECAUSE THERE HE FELT VERY QUICKLY THAT NO ONE ACCEPTED HIM. HE WAS ALONE, ALONE IN A CITY OF MILLIONS. EVENTUALLY HE BEGAN TO DIARY TO LEAD, TO WRITE

HIS HATRED OF THE SOUL. OF COURSE, HE HAD TO HIDE THE BOOK WELL. HE WAS ALONE AT HOME, THE FACILITY TURNED FULLY ON AND WRITE GEBANN. FUELED BY THE SOUND HE COULD NOT STOP WRITING, THE WORDS JUST POURED OUT:

"TODAY IS THE DAY WHERE I FINALLY WANT TO WIPE THE SLATE CLEAN. MIKE AND HIS GANG HAVE MADE ME THIS MORNING AGAIN FINISHED. THEY LAUGHED

AT ME, NUDGED ME. NOW IS SETTLED ... "

SO FOR NOW IT WAS ENOUGH, HE KNEW WHAT TO DO. IN HIS MIND HE SAW THEM ALREADY ALL LIE THERE. NOT A BAD WORD HE WOULD HEAR MORE, NOTHING WOULD TORMENT HIM MORE. IN ADDITION, HERE IN AMERICA, IT IS NORMAL THAT THE KIDS ANYWAY SOMEDAY RUN AMOK OR? HE SAW IN HIS MIND'S EYE, AS HE LET FLY

THE YELLOW IRON PIPE ON THE SKULLS OF PEOPLE OVER AND OVER AGAIN. YOU FINALLY GOT WHAT THEY DESERVED. WELL HIDDEN, HE HAD THE IRON ROD, HE DID NOT WANT THE CLICHE CORRESPOND NOT TO GET HUGE SUMS FOR WEAPONS AND THEN WILD TO SHOOT HIMSELF. NO, SOMETIME HE FOUND ON HIS WAY HOME FROM SCHOOL ARE THE HEAVY IRON PIECE ON THE FLOOR, HEEDLESS SOMEONE HAD CHUCKED. IT FIT JUST SO IN HIS SPORTS

BAG, NO ONE GOT WITH THAT HE LIFTED HER EYE. THEN HE LOOKED FOR A SUITABLE HIDING PLACE. HE PUT THE DIARY AMONG HIS PAPERS, CLOSED THE DRAWER, BUT THEN IT MADE BREAK. HE LISTENED MORE CLOSELY, TURNED THE MUSIC DOWN, WHAT WAS THAT? IT WAS A FEELING THAT TRIGGERED BY THE MUSIC, MOTIVATED HIM TO GO INTO THE KITCHEN AND HOLFEN THE NEWSPAPER. THEN HE TURNED PALE. HE READ THE REPORT ON

YOUNG PEOPLE WHO HAVE A MASSACRE SERVED AT A SCHOOL. IT HAS BEEN SPECULATED THAT ONE OF THE REASONS THE MUSIC WOULD BE. AND THAT WAS EXACTLY THE ONE HE HEARS. SURROUNDED BY BAD IMAGES, GRUESOME, HE WOKE UP AT LAST. HE WOULD NEVER USE HIS IRON BAR TO HURT PEOPLE. HE FELL TO HIS KNEES, WITH A PRAYER ASKING FORGIVENESS FOR ALL HIS SINS AND SPEAKING MAINLY FOR WHAT HE

WANTED TO DO AT THE PRESENT DAY. HE SWITCHED THE SYSTEM OFF, WENT TO THE HIDING PLACE, TOOK THE IRON BAR AND THREW IT INTO THE DUSTBIN. IT HAS BEEN OBSERVED AND THAT ANNOYED HIM. THAT WAS THE BEGINNING OF THE FRIENDSHIP BETWEEN BAD PET AND X, WHICH BROUGHT HIM TO THE WG WHERE THINGS GET LIVELY, A FAMOUS URBANIZATION.

ALL RESIDENTS OF WG PLAY THEMSELVES IN THE SENSE OF ALL ASSUME THEIR WORK AS USUAL, MUSIC, WRITING, ART, FASHION AND FASHION SHOW, WHICH WILL BE SNAPPED BY THE PHOTOGRAPHER.

SUDDENLY THE DOORBELL RINGS AND ALIEN IS THERE. THE MEMBERS OF THE WG BELIEVE THAT ALIEN WEARING A SUIT FOR EXAMPLE, A MUSICIAN

OCCURS, HE WAS LOOKING FOR AN APARTMENT, OF COURSE, ALL IMMEDIATELY STARTED TALKING.

ALIEN TELLS OF HIS PAST WHEN HE WAS ALONG WITH LENA, PLAYED BY KIRA. SHE WAS BLIND AND ALIEN A RESEARCHER WHO HAS SPENT HIS LIFE IN THE BOARDING SCHOOL - HIS PARENTS HAVE A BABY BORN THAT LOOKS LIKE THIS. HOW COULD HE EVER INTEGRATE? IN RETROSPECT REMEMBERS

ALIENS FATHER, PLAYED BY NICK SICK ABOUT THE ATROCITIES THAT HAD TO ENDURE AT SCHOOL. THEY TRIED HIS FACE CUT OPEN TO SEE WHAT'S UNDERNEATH. HIS PARENTS RESEARCHED AND FOUND A SCHOOL, A BOARDING SCHOOL, WITH

AMAZING CHILDREN. THERE FELT ALIEN AND PROBABLY ALSO DISCOVERED HIS PASSION FOR SCIENCE AND RESEARCH, BUT ALSO MUSIC, BECAUSE AS A

MUSICIAN YOU CAN CALMLY LOOK CRAZY.

HIS GIRLFRIEND LENA, WHO IS BLIND, WAS NOT ABLE TO LIVE IN THE FLAT, BECAUSE IT IS NOT RIGHTS FOR HUMAN BEINGS FURNISHINGS. LENA WAS BLIND FROM BIRTH, SINCE WOULD BE TO DO NOTHING. BUT ALIEN DID NOT GIVE UP. HE WORKED IN A LABORATORY, STUDIED WITH SCHOLARS AT THE LATEST TECHNICAL EQUIPMENT, BUT ALSO TO

SOFTWARE - EVERYTHING RELATES TO DIGITAL MEDIA. THROUGH HIS KNOWLEDGE DEVELOPED ALIEN CONTACT LENSES ARE INSIDE WHICH FINEST NEURAL HELPERS. AT THE SAME TIME CAME OUT THE MACHINE THAT CONJURES FROM A NORMAL ROOM SEA.

SCENE CHANGE

THE WG IS IN THE CITY NOT TO DISTURB THE YOUNG COUPLE. IN THE CITY WAS CULTURAL FAIR AND

SUDDENLY THEY SAW A WOMAN WHO ACCOMPLISHED ACROBATIC PERFORMANCE. AFTER THE SHOW THEY GET IN CONTACT WITH SIRA.

CHANGE OF SCENE IN THE HOUSE OF WG

THERE ARE ALIEN AND HIS GIRLFRIEND LENA. BOTH EXPERIENCE THE BEACH LIFE LIKE IN THE CARIBBEAN. LENA WANTED NOTHING MORE IN THE WORLD, AS WELL AS BEING ABLE TO SEE, TO LIVE A NORMAL LIFE. HE TOLD LENA THAT THEY SHOULD

PUT THE CONTACT LENSES, WHICH SHE DID. AND SHE COULD SEE DIRECTLY, TURNED AROUND, SAW THE PALM TREES AND THE FIRST TIME ALIEN YOUR FRIEND. SHE TOOK HER BAG AND WENT, SHE WAS NO LONGER ACCESSIBLE. FOR THE SCIENTIST, A WORLD COLLAPSED. HOWEVER, SHORTLY AFTER THE TRAGEDY CAME HOME THE OTHER.

END OF TREATMENT, WHICH ALSO MAY HAVE A SECOND PART.

THE CUTE PETS LEARNED THEIR ROLES, WHICH WERE QUITE NATURAL, ALMOST ALL WERE HER NORMAL LIFE AS USUAL IN THE FILM.

SOME SCENES LIKE THE THE NOT TAKEN PLACE AMOK THE MASSACRE APPEARS ON THE COMOMBINE HIGH SCHOOL.

THAT IS THE FILM-

... TO BE CONTINUED

THE FILM IS MUCH MORE ACTION. IT WAS SUMMER AND THE FILM CAME IN THE CINEMA IN PETCITY. AFTER WORK WITH THIS FILM THE ACTORS – KIRA BIEN AND HER HUSBAND NICK SICK – STARS AND CELEBRITIES FLYING AWAY - HOLLYWOOD IS WAITING. NOW IT IS COLD OUTSIDE, EVERYTHING LOOKS LIKE A

OLD BLACK AND WHITE FILM. NOBODY OUTSIDE KNOWS ABOUT THE WORK FOR THIS FILM IN PETCITY, BUT AFTER THE FILM WAS PUBLISHED, THE NEWSPAPER RUNNING TO THE CUTE PETS. THE ONE AND ONLY QUESTION EVER: WHAT ARE YOU DOING WITH THE MONEY? ANGELA, HER HUSBAND ALIEN, MAEHI & HIS WIFE ANGELINA, GOOD PET & HIS WIFE HAESCHEN, MICHELLE AND HER HUSBAND X, AMBER, SAMMY AND KITTY DON'T

TALK ABOUT THIS THEME. THE TRUTH IS: ALL 11 CUTE PETS LAY THEIR MONEY ON THE TABLE, NOBODY HAS MONEY ON CARDS, BANK. STEP 1: EVERYBODY TALKS ABOUT THE PERSONAL SITUATION, WHICH IS PERHAPS CONNECTED WITH PROBLEMS AND EVERYBODY OF THE GROUP GETS THE MONEY TO SOLVE PROBLEMS.

STEP 2: AMBER HAS A ON CHARITY LIKE THE SOCIAL PROJECT, WHERE THE

FAMILY OF KITTY – MR. AND MRS. FEILER MAKE AND THE INSTITUTION OF THE FAMOUS GIRL, WHICH ALSO HAS WRITTEN A KITTY SONG.

SAMMY HAS PROJECTS EVERYWHERE IN THE WORLD.

STEP 3: MONEY FOR THE WORK – THE CUTE PETS ARE A BAND, WRITING BOOKS, DESIGN FASHION, ART, SCIENCES, CHARITY EVENTS

STEP 4: THE REST IS FOR PERSONAL USING. EVERY OF THE 11 PEOPLE GETS 1000 $. WHAT WOULD THE JOURNALIST SAY, WHEN THE CUTE PETS EXPLAIN, THAT EVERYBODY HAS 1000 $ ON A SECRET PLACE. LOLL. WOULD THE JOURNALIST BELIEVE THIS? OR LAUGHING THE WORLD ABOUT THE COMMUNITY?

THE TELEPHONE IS RINGING

IT IS NOVEMBER, DEPRESSION AND WHERE IS THE MONEY? SUDDENLY THE TELEPHONE IS RINGING - KIRA BIEN AND NICK SICK ARE IN TOWN FOR A VIEW MINUTES, BECAUSE THEY WANT MAKE HOLIDAYS IN PARIS. MICHELLE AND X RUNNING TO THE CINEMA, THE OTHERS FEELING SICK. AFTER TEN MINUTES KIRA BIEN, NICK SICK, MICHELLE AND X ARE TOGETHER,

LOOKING AT THE CINEMA PICTURE FOR THE FILM "AMERICAN STORY". ONLY A SHORT MEETING IS POSSIBLE, TOP SECRET MEETING. NICK AND KIRA ARE STARS, EVERYBODY WHO LIVES IN PETCITY WOULD GO TO THE CINEMA FOR A SIGNATURE, MAKING PICTURES. DAM - KIRA & NICK DON'T HAVE A HANDY IN HOLIDAYS AND MICHELLE FORGET THE HANDY FOR MAKING A PIC. BUT NO PROBLEM, A WOMAN - SHE DOESN'T KNOW THAT SHE IS

TALKING WITH HOLLYWOOD STARS – HAD A CAMERA. A OLD OLD OLD CAMERA, WHICH GIVES YOU DIRECTLY THE PICTURE AFTER MAKING. AMAZING. SHE MAKES A SNAPSHOT –

A HALF OUR LATER MICHELLE AND X ARE AT HOME, SHOWING THE PIC. GREAT SURPRISE. KITTY IS EXCITED – BUM THE COFFEE IS ON THE IMAGE. NOW THEY HAVE A VINTAGE PIC. ☺

I SAY THANK YOU TO MY HUSBAND

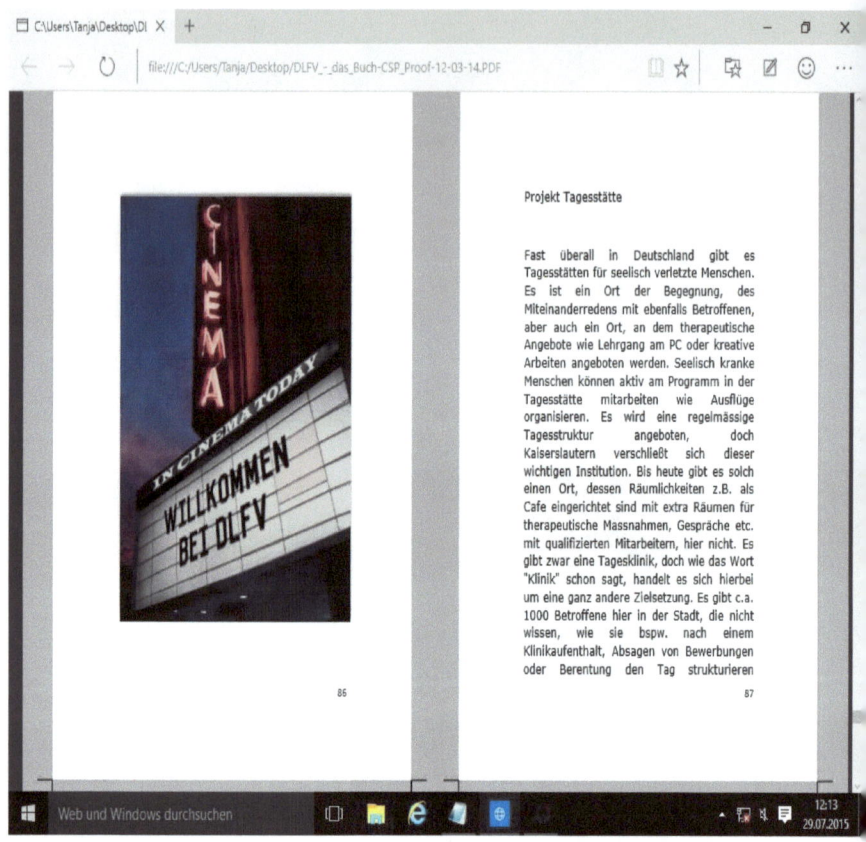

THE SOCIAL PROJECT MR. AND MRS. FEILER

SING THE CHRISTMAS SONG ALL DAY LONG